DEDICATION

This book is dedicated to my dear cousin, Moira, who has been such an important part of my life for so many years.

THANKS

My grateful thanks to my most excellent friend, Pam Baillie. She is able to spot a rogue apostrophe or misplaced exclamation mark in Cheltenham from her home deep in the Scottish Highlands. Remarkable! Her support, encouragement, advice and forensic editorial eye have been invaluable.

COVER PICTURE

The cover picture is of the parade ring at York just before the running of the Juddmonte International in August 2009. I had gone there with friends especially to see the imperious Sea The Stars run. He did not disappoint!

INTRODUCTION

Racecourse Rhymes is a collection of limericks. At the beginning of the 3rd Lockdown, in early January 2021, I challenged myself to write one for every racecourse in Great Britain, of which there are currently 59. I am both surprised and delighted to have completed the set!

A few of my limericks are about the characteristics of a course or its location. But most are about racing people and incidents that could have happened anywhere - the name of the course and words that it rhymes with being an important determining factor.

Racing attracts larger-than-life characters and its swiftly-changing fortunes inevitably heighten emotions and seed eccentric behaviour. Throw in the effects of over-imbibing (sadly not unknown) and the sometimes uneasy relationships between the various participants in the sport, and there is a rich source of material to work with. It is also undeniably true that winning is not funny but misfortune is, and you will find many reflections of that basic fact in these pages.

Racing is also a rich source of stories - and here is mine. A few years ago, I was in The Queen's Hotel late on Friday night after the last day of the Cheltenham Festival, by which time everyone is very ragged. I was in the Gents when two Irishmen, who clearly did not know each other, walked in. One said, “Did you have a good Festival?”. The other replied, “Fantastic”. The first chap then said, “You must have had a few winners?” “No”, the second chap replied, “Not a single one, but it was great craic.”

I always try to recall this man’s admirable attitude whenever I lose – which is frequently! This may be partly because I am too lazy to study form and love words, so I often back horses by name. But every dog has his day and mine was 16 October 2015 when I put an each-way multiple on horses called Debit, Balance, Scrutiny, Modest, Zealous and Regulation simply because they seemed such inappropriate names for horses. My £12.60 investment paid £1500.70. Yippee!

So, to return neatly to the subject, this book definitely represents my best chance of making a few bob out of racing. But mostly, I hope it provides a few laughs to those of you who still retain the ability to laugh at yourselves in these tough times.

MS

LUDLOW

At Ludlow, a young chap I found

Said, “I want to put on a pound.

If I back it each-way

And it wins, will it pay,

No matter which way it goes round?”

SANDOWN

At Sandown my horse was just gliding –

What a race the jockey was riding!

At the famed railway fences

He lost all his senses

And rode right off into a siding!

UTTOXETER

Sometimes at Uttoxeter, Staffs,

A jockey will make a few gaffes.

If he returns muddied

Or, even worse, bloodied –

Don't ask him to sign autographs!

SALISBURY

A man went to Salisbury Races

But had sadly forgotten his braces.

He jumped more than most

As his horse passed the post –

Now he's waiting to know when his case is!

WETHERBY

Will Shakespeare wrote with such perfection

But here’s a humble new suggestion –

Wetherby

Or not to be

Surely that should be the question?

PLUMPTON

Plumpton sounds so very posh

Is it full of gels all saying ‘Gosh’?

One thing’s for certain

If you've got a skirt on

The bookies will still take your dosh.

TAUNTON

Said a lady at Taunton racecourse,
"My old fella has lost all his force.
He needs something quick,
Perhaps gelding's the trick?
Well, it seemed to work for my horse!"

STRATFORD-UPON-AVON

At Stratford – home of the Bard,
Romeo looked at the card
And backed Juliet,
She's still running yet –
Betting is ever so hard!

CHESTER

There once was a lady at Chester

Who wore only a yellow sou'wester.

When she went racing –

She found it quite bracing

But the police still had to arrest her!

AINTREE

When Aintree Ladies Day commences

Some Scouser girls can lose their senses.

A nervous man

May find fake tan

Is scarier than the National Fences!

WARWICK

An actor friend once said to me,
"Self-confidence is the key.
When you go to Warwick
Say you knew poor Yorick –
They might let you go in for free!"

YORK

At York you can't get owt for nowt
And beware when casting a clout,
Look after thy lass,
Hang on to thy brass,
Those are the rules hereabout!

PERTH

A chap by the paddock at Perth

Said to his pal (just in mirth?)

“If I stay for the last

I must get away fast –

My wife's just about to give birth!"

FFOS LAS

The day that I went to Ffos Las

I slipped and fell tip over ass.

A mate said, "I think

It could be the drink –

Why not just try one more glass?"

HEXHAM

Do the ladies at Hexham wear heather?

Are they stout or as light as a feather?

These questions and more

I would like to explore

But it rather depends on the weather!

PONTEFRACT

When going up to Pontefract

Please beware of this one fact –

Too much of the cake

Can make your tum ache

And leave your lips sort of blacked!

AYR

A canny horse owner at Ayr

Accosted a young English pair,

“He was held back today

But he'll win going away –

Would you like to purchase a share?”

BANGOR-ON-DEE

A fellow at Bangor-on-Dee

Went on an immense betting spree.

He backed every horse –

Had the winners, of course –

And a debit of 35p!

WINDSOR

You're at Windsor on a boat trip
And have spotted a handicap snip.
If the horse doesn't win
Please don't jump in
Just repair to the bar for a nip!

NOTTINGHAM

At Nottingham, try as I could
To see the trees from the wood,
I looked all in vain,
Again and again,
For a bookmaker named Robin Hood!

NEWBURY

We’re at Newbury on a freebie

But my missus still bets 50p

So the wages of sin

Are terribly thin

And they won't pay for dinner for me!

DONCASTER

One race-day a nurse at Doncaster

Had to put a jockey in plaster.

He said, "After it's done,

How about a quick one?"

A question he shouldn't have asked her!

CHELTENHAM

In March at Cheltenham Spa

Jumps lovers come from afar.

The Irish are tops

The craic never stops –

For one week it’s Cheltenham Bar!

BATH

At Bath, one evening, the vicar

Boasted, "Bishop, my nag is much quicker –

Oh curse upon curse,

It's gone into reverse!

There goes my last twenty nicker!"

EXETER

At Exeter, on a day trip,

I heard a young stable lass quip,

“Though the wages are bad,

There's fun to be had

In the world of leather and whip!”

FONTWELL PARK

Fontwell’s a tricky old track

Where jockeys must master the knack –

Not all of them hate

Its figure of eight

But some meet themselves coming back!

LINGFIELD PARK

A young fellow whose ears were still wet
Went to Lingfield to get out of debt.
“I'm only a rookie,”
He said to a bookie,
“Can you tell me which horse I should bet?”

KEMPTON PARK

An owner I'd better not mention
Complained to his trainer at Kempton,
"I've won bugger-all
‘Cos my horse had a fall."
"Oh, let’s call it hyper-extension!”

ASCOT

When you wear a top hat to Ascot
Some might think you have got a big yacht
With a model for crew,
Plus a Bentley or two,
But you've hired it more often than not!

BRIGHTON

At Brighton, this public school toff
Chatters a lot while he quaffs
And likes a late bet
But he hasn’t learned yet –
"Sorry, old chap, they're just off!”

RIPON

At Ripon, a tough female trainer

Said, "Jockey, I couldn't speak plainer –

Are thee owt good in bed?"

He sheepishly said,

“I'm only a seven pound claimer!”

KELSO

At Kelso, in Roxburghshire,

A tipsy chap caused such a stir.

“They won't pay me out,”

He started to shout.

"But the race hasn’t started yet, Sir!"

BEVERLEY

In the grandstand at old Beverley,

A chap kissed a girl, covertly.

His wife – who was fiery –

Said, "Stewards' Enquiry

As soon as we get home for tea!"

SOUTHWELL

One race-day at Southwell, in Notts,

I backed all the jocks wearing spots,

A dubious plan

That went down the pan –

So next time I'll try drawing lots!

WORCESTER

At Worcester, a jockey walked by

And said to a lady, "Can I

Please ride your best horse?"

She said, "You've got a sauce,"

Which was such a witty reply!

NEWTON ABBOT

At Newton Abbot in Devon –

The county some say is in heaven –

A daft friend of mine

Always carries a sign

Saying, ‘Free the ITV Seven!’

REDCAR

At Redcar, by the paddock one day,

A mate heard a drunk punter say,

To the No. 4 horse,

“You will win, of course.”

But the animal just answered, "Neigh!”

NEWMARKET

Newmarket's the home of the horse

And has famously got one more course

Than the rest,

But which one is best?

Perhaps it is just horse for course!

HUNTINGDON

On a race-day at old Huntingdon
I was counting out what I had won
When my French girlfriend spake,
“Thank you, zis I vill take –
I have, in ze oven, a bun!”

CARLISLE

On the day that I went to Carlisle
A young lady on the turnstile
Said, "If you marry me,
You can go in for free."
I politely declined - with a smile!

CHELMSFORD

At Chelmsford, once known as Great Leighs,
A chap felt a certain unease –
When his girlfriend took whisky
She quite often turned frisky
And usually did a striptease!

THIRSK

My girlfriend and I play a game –
I study: she chooses by name.
One bad day at Thirsk,
All her horses came first
And most of mine finished quite lame!

CATTERICK

In a bumper at old Catterick

My gee-gee went off mighty quick –

I was over the moon

But, sadly, too soon,

And now, as a parrot, I'm sick!

GREAT YARMOUTH

One day at Great Yarmouth perchance

My selection sweated and pranced.

"Can it still win?"

I said to my twin.

He just said, "It’s got Norfolk and chance!”

HEREFORD

On a soggy, wet Valentine's Day,

A young chap took his girlfriend away

To Hereford – racing –

A day's hunter-chasing –

It's over now, needless to say!

HAYDOCK PARK

One day when I went to Haydock

My horse's defeat was a shock

But my (ex) trainer's reason –

The horse was in season –

Was rubbish – 'cos I saw its cock!

WINCANTON

"Though it certainly cannot be blamed,

Wincanton is not aptly named –

Losscanton would be

More fitting for me!"

One unhappy punter proclaimed.

LEICESTER

"King Richard the Third," said one source,

"Would have swapped his land for a horse."

One day at Leicester

A silly investor

Also tried this most unwise recourse!

CARTMEL

The lovely course at Cartmel

Comes with its very own fell

Which is both iconic,

And sadly ironic –

'Cos my bloody horse fell there as well!

HAMILTON PARK

One evening at Hamilton Park

A man made this silly remark,

"If I want to get skewered,

Should I look for a steward?

And why does the course need a clerk?"

SEDGEFIELD

The day that I went to Sedgefield

I met a smart girl who appealed,

"Do I have a chance

Of instant romance?"

"You do if you're very well-heeled!"

NEWCASTLE

To avoid embarrassed red faces

When going to the Newcastle Races,

If a chap says, 'Howay,'

He might just mean, 'Good day!'

So please don't get all airs and graces!

WOLVERHAMPTON

Wolverhampton’s an all-weather track,

Where Black Country folk go for the craic.

“It’s not The Savoy,”

Said one local old boy,

“But I always keeps coming back!”

CHEPSTOW

At Chepstow, a young jockey I knew,

When asked, "Why d’you do what you do?"

Delayed for a while

Then said, with a smile,

"I just like wearing silks. Wouldn't you?"

MUSSELBURGH

At Musselburgh I heard a chap tell

How his horse had jinked, stumbled and fell.

"I wouldnae mind that,"

He said (sounding flat)

"But the Rangers were beaten as well!"

GOODWOOD

Goodwood's a glorious place

Where racehorses glide with such grace

To great fame and renown

On that lush Sussex down –

Though mine frequently sink without trace!

MARKET RASEN

When you're betting at far Market Rasen,

A study of horse conformation

May well do the trick

But I think I'll just stick

To a safe algebraic equation!

FAKENHAM

Tenners – this fella kept making 'em

To racetracks he would keep on taking 'em.

When caught in possession

The cop said, "One question –

Was it really so wise to choose Fakenham?"

EPSOM

To Epsom Downs for the Derby bash

Londoners come with bangers and mash –

A score on the winner

Then off to Frank Skinner,

Some King Lears and a Mark Ramprakash!

Cockney rhyming slang

bangers and mash = cash, score = £20, Frank Skinner = dinner, King Lears = beers and Mark Ramprakash = what you need after several King Lears!

ALSO BY ME

If you would like to read something completely different, I have also published a collection of satirical verse, song parodies and other silliness mainly about lockdown life and politics. It is called **The Lockdown Verses** and is available from Amazon for the price of a London pint.

Printed in Poland
by Amazon Fulfillment
Poland Sp. z o.o., Wrocław

88437619R00020